God's Compassion Towards Me

Mental Health Professionals
Share Wisdom...
How God's Compassion Flows
Through Them To Others

Edited by
Dr. Lisa H. Fuller

Published by
Learn Realistic Habits for the Future

God's Compassion Towards Me

Copyright © 2023 Learn Realistic Habits for the Future

All Scriptures are taken from the King James Version of the Bible (KJV)

All rights reserved.
ISBN 13: 978-0-9754023-6-8 – Print
ISBN 13: 979-8-9886371-1-0 – Ebook

Editor: Dr. Lisa H. Fuller

In collaboration with Lisa H. Fuller Ministries

Cover and Layout Design: Christina Dixon

Table of Contents

Disclaimers .... *i*

Introduction 1

Chapter 1: God's Compassion on Me – Dr. Hellen Njoroge 5

Chapter 2: Destruction of the Soul – Dr. Lisa G. Brooks 19

Chapter 3: Inner Turmoil – Doctoral Candidate Courtney Cabell 31

Chapter 4: Not Good Enough – Dr. Bronwyn Davis 41

Chapter 5: It's Never Too Late – Dr. Chlorine Wimberly 55

Reflection 69

About the Editor – Dr. Lisa H Fuller 71

Disclaimers

God's Compassion Towards Me does not represent any form of diagnosis, treatment, recommendation, or advice. God's Compassion Towards Me is intended for informational purposes only.

If reading God's Compassion Towards Me precipitates any triggers, flashbacks, emotional responses, etc. contact and follow-up with mental and/or medical health professionals. If you are a threat to yourself or others, contact 911 OR 988. 988 is a 24-hour Suicide and Crisis Lifeline. (No affiliation with 911 or 988.)

Stop reading God's Compassion Towards Me if you do not accept all parts of this disclaimer.

NOTE: The authors of this book are educated Christian believers who are aware that proper nouns should begin with capital letters. However, as a literary demonstration of their faith that Jesus Christ reigns triumphant over the works of the devil, readers of this book will notice that the name satan is not capitalized.

Introduction

The World Health Organization estimates one in four people globally will experience mental illness in their lifetime. Furthermore, Mental Health America, reports in 2022 approximately 50 million Americans experienced mental illness. Mental illness is a real and serious illness. Several people experiencing mental illness may never receive treatment. Mental illness can worsen over time to the point the effects devastate one's life if not addressed resulting in broken relationships, job termination due to reduced and unmet productivity, social isolation and loneliness, health challenges (reduced immunity, ending remission of terminal illnesses, headaches, fatigue, abdominal discomfort), addictions, sleep interruption, appetite changes, suicidal thoughts, and completed suicide resulting in death.

I ask the following questions when speaking to various groups and talking to my patients. If you had chest pain or chest heaviness, where would you go? Where would you go if your leg was profusely bleeding from a deep cut sustained from a fall while walking your dog? Where would you go if your nose was profusely bleeding for 10 minutes? Where would you go if you experienced food poisoning? Where would you go if you fainted or blacked out? Answer: To the emergency department, urgent care, or your primary care physician's office seeking treatment.

Being apprehensive when receiving mental health treatment, especially for the first time, is normal. The truth be told, anxiety or apprehension when receiving any treatment can be a normal reaction. It is awkward to discuss with someone you don't know your innermost and deep seeded problems, most embarrassing moments, sustained disappointments, or trauma.

God's Compassion Towards Me

God heals by miracles, signs, and wonders...over time...by using clinicians. In Christian counseling sessions, there are three people, the person receiving counseling, the provider, and the Holy Spirit.

MYTHS

- "Mental illness is a lack of willpower. It is not a real illness."
- "Mental illness is a character weakness."
- "All you need to do is be strong."
- "You need to pray more."
- "You don't have enough faith."
- "All they do is drug you. You will never be the same."
- "People with a mental illness cannot work."
- "People with mental illness cannot live independently in the community."
- "They are violent."

TRUTHS and FACTS

- Mental illness is a real disease.
- An individual diagnosed with mental illness has the right to agree or disagree with prescribed medication unless court ordered for the person's and other's safety.
- A diagnosis of mental illness does not automatically eliminate an individual from working.
- Diagnosis of a mental illness does not necessarily prohibit a person from living independently.
- Not all people with mental illnesses are violent.
- Believers in the body of Christ receive counseling and therapy.

Introduction

- Christian, Holy Spirit-filled counselors, psychologists, and psychiatrists exist.

FACT

God heals, restores, and transforms by

...miracles, signs, & wonders

...over time and

...through Spirit-filled clinicians.

God's Compassion Towards Me is a compilation of five Spirit-filled professional mental health clinicians who share their own stories and how God empowers them to help others.

Beloved, I wish above all things that thou mayest prosper and be in health, even as thy soul prospereth. III John 3:2.

Dr. Lisa H. Fuller

Chapter 1:
God's Compassion on Me

God's compassion for me is what gives me the strength, hope, and faith to keep going, even when I feel like giving up. From a perspective of mental health and faith, God shows up in various ways when our mental states are messed up (Kristeller & Johnson, 2005). Firstly, God offers comfort and solace through prayer, scripture, and community support. Additionally, seeking professional help from mental health experts is an important step toward healing, and God's compassion can be present through the provision of such professional assistance.

God has been compassionate to me by providing me with strength and comfort during difficult times. In moments of stress, anxiety, or grief, many people find solace in prayer or meditation, turning to their faith for support and guidance (Crawford et al., 2006). Through this connection with God, I may feel a sense of calm, hope, and reassurance, knowing that I am not alone and that a higher power is watching over me. Many religious traditions promote the values of kindness, compassion, and forgiveness, which inspire me to show these qualities to others. This often leads to experiences that are more positive and the best emotions. Ultimately, experiencing God's compassion is a personal and subjective experience, and may take many different forms based on individual beliefs and experiences (Crawford et al., 2006).

In an era of endangered gender-based violence (Reese Masterson, 2013), a woman was brought into a health support department. Her face was destroyed. Her experience of how her husband burned her face was fresh in her mind. The least she expected was to be alive today. How could it be possible that someone saved her? The hospital paid a whopping bill. The doctors treated her successfully. Would this be the compassion of God? Yes, it is completely the compassion of God. Who would sustain a broken heart and life as such? In his intervention through the doctors, he showed his mercy to the woman, to keep her alive once again.

It reminds me of a woman named Sarah who had been suffering from heart disease for several years. Despite her condition, Sarah always tried to maintain a positive attitude and believed that she could overcome her illness. However, things took a turn for the worse when her heart disease started to cause complications in her kidneys and lungs, and she was admitted to the hospital for treatment. For three months, Sarah was unable to walk and could not eat anything due to her failing health. She felt like giving up hope and succumbing to her illness, but one day she heard a voice in her heart that spoke to her. The voice was soothing and reassuring, and it told Sarah that all the diseases that had come along with her heart disease would be healed.

The voice also told her that this was her testimony of the mercy and compassion of God to her, and that she needed to make a choice to live in faith and dwell in the compassion of God. Sarah was overwhelmed with emotion and felt a sense of peace and comfort that she had never experienced. In addition, she saw the smile of Jesus that reassured her of gratitude and hope.

From that day on, Sarah chose to believe in the healing power of God and put all her trust in Him. She started to recite prayers and read scriptures daily and slowly but surely, her health started to improve. Her kidneys and lungs began to function properly, and she was able to walk and eat normally again.

Chapter 1: God's Compassion on Me

Sarah knew that it was only through the grace and mercy of God that she had been healed, and she felt a deep sense of gratitude towards Him. She made a promise to herself to continue living in faith and to share her testimony with others who were going through difficult times. In the end, Sarah's experience taught her that no matter how dire the situation may seem, there is always hope and that the power of faith and trust in God can bring about miracles.

To build up faith to maintain good mental health, it is essential to prioritize self-care, such as developing healthy coping mechanisms and setting boundaries. Practicing gratitude, and meditation can also be helpful in promoting mental wellness and strengthening one's relationship with God. Surrounding oneself with a supportive faith community can provide a sense of belonging and encouragement during difficult times.

To take hold of the compassion of God on us, it is important to cultivate a sense of trust in God's plan and purpose for our lives, the battle is the Lord's (Barton, 2018). This can be achieved by regularly reading and meditating on scripture, as well as engaging in prayer and worship. Remembering that God's love is unconditional and not based on our performance can also provide comfort and assurance during challenging seasons of life. "Though the mountains be shaken and the hills be removed, yet my unfailing love for you will not be shaken nor my covenant of peace be removed," says the Lord, who has compassion on you (Isaiah 54:10).

Aristotle in Nicomachean Ethics makes a proposition of virtue and the creation of a means between extremes. It is inevitable that in our daily endeavors, the earth will break loose. We get our mental stability put to the test (Solmsen, 1964). For the absence of anger aimed at a right offense is a vice rather than a virtue. However, the divine test of our mental abilities is our ease to recognize the compassion of God. To listen to His silent voice that whispers deep into our infinite mind, to moderate our extremes, emotions, and reason, and find a means to enable us not to derail in pain, in addition not also to sink in ignorance of the existence of the pain. Rather, discern the compassion of God and lie close to him for consolation.

I have worked with clients who identify with the Christian faith, but have often found that their faith and mental health do not sit at the same table, leading them to question – "Does God care about how I am feeling, my depression or anxiety?" "Is it okay to take anxiety medication?" "Is my depression due to a lack of faith?" I find solace in going directly to God. This passage in Matthew teaches that my thoughts and the state of my mental health matter to God (Matthew 22:37). He asks me to love him with my entire mind. He is interested in my thoughts, emotions, and ideas. How? How does one love God with the mind? Paul writes in Romans 12:2, "…be transformed by the renewing of your mind." Renewing our minds is the way to transformation; it is a way that we love God with our minds (Schoonover-Shoffner, 2016). In another Scripture, St Paul speaking to the Philippians said, "Be careful for nothing; but in every thing by prayer and supplication with thanksgiving let your requests be made known unto God. And the peace of God, which passeth all understanding, shall keep your hearts and minds through Christ Jesus." (Philippians 4:6-7).

Suffering is a universal experience, so church leaders need to be well-equipped to care for people who are going through hardship. When you have walked with God through something as difficult as depression, it gives you a greater ability to walk with others through

Chapter 1: God's Compassion on Me

difficult times. Not only can depression increase a person's level of compassion and empathy, but it can also provide a new perspective on life that equips them for Christian leadership. Personally, when I was depressed, my prayer life increased. I needed God in a way I never had before. In some moments, all I could do was pray, "God, help everything to be okay." Nevertheless, I knew He was there, sustaining me when I did not have the ability to sustain myself.

God's influence on our mental health

God's influence on our mental health is undeniable. He is the one who gives us the strength to keep going and never give up. He is the one who gives us the courage to face our fears and to keep believing in ourselves. God's protection, comfort, and influence on our mental health are what give us the strength, hope, and faith to keep going and to never give up even though we feel like giving up. God is always there to protect us and provide us with comfort (Tan & Gregg, 2010). He is the one who gives us the courage to face our fears and to keep believing in ourselves. The concept of God and spirituality can have a profound impact on mental wellness for many individuals.

Ways God may influence our mental wellness:

Sense of purpose and meaning:

Believing in a higher power can provide a sense of purpose and meaning in life, which can contribute to feelings of contentment and fulfillment.

Coping with stress and anxiety:

Faith in God can provide comfort and support during difficult times and can help individuals cope with stress and anxiety.

God's Compassion Towards Me

Social support:

Participation in a religious community can provide social support and a sense of belonging, which can improve mental wellness.

Forgiveness:

Many religious beliefs promote forgiveness and compassion, which can improve relationships and reduce negative emotions such as anger and resentment.

Gratitude:

Recognizing and expressing gratitude for blessings and positive experiences can improve overall well-being and promote positive thinking. It is important to note that while faith and spirituality can have a positive impact on mental wellness for some individuals; this may not be true for everyone. Each individual's beliefs and experiences are unique, and the relationship between spirituality and mental wellness can be complex and multifaceted.

Connected to God in my mental wellness

The ultimate friend we find in our pain is Jesus Himself. He wept for us. In addition, on the Cross, He experienced separation from God in its fullness. Our Savior knows what it means to suffer darkness. It is not uncommon for people to feel a connection to a higher power or God as a source of comfort and support in their mental wellness journey. This connection can provide a sense of purpose, meaning, and hope, which can be particularly helpful during challenging times.

The ways I nurture and deepen my connection to God in my mental wellness journey; include practices such as:

Chapter 1: God's Compassion on Me

- **Prayer:** Talking to God through prayer can be a powerful way to express your thoughts, feelings, and concerns.
- **Meditation:** Taking time to quiet your mind and focus on God through meditation can help you feel more connected and centered.
- **Reading religious or spiritual texts:** Many people find solace and guidance in reading religious or spiritual texts, such as the Bible (Everyday Health, n.d.).
- **Attending religious services:** Participating in religious services, such as church, can provide a sense of community and support.
- **Practicing gratitude:** Focusing on the blessings in your life and expressing gratitude to God can help you cultivate a more positive mindset.

It is important to remember that everyone's journey is unique, and what works for one person may not work for another. If you find that connecting to God in your mental wellness journey is not helpful or meaningful to you that is okay too. It's important to find what works best for you and to seek support from mental health professionals if needed.

However, when you are experiencing a mental health crisis and feeling isolated, it is very easy to forget that God is literally within you. The Holy Spirit is the presence of God Himself, living and active in the life of everyone who trusts in God. When Jesus was about to be arrested and crucified, He sensed the distress among His closest followers. He knew the crisis they were about to go through. His solution was to reveal to them that their very reality as individual humans was about to be transformed in an unprecedented way.

God's Compassion Towards Me

"I have yet many things to say unto you, but ye cannot bear them now. Howbeit when he, the Spirit of truth, is come, he will guide you into all truth: for he shall not speak of himself; but whatsoever he shall hear, that shall he speak: and he will shew you things to come. He shall glorify me: for he shall receive of mine, and shall shew it unto you. All things that the Father hath are mine: therefore said I, that he shall take of mine, and shall shew it unto you." (St. John 16:12-15)

Some individuals believe that God is engaged in the world, functioning as a positive force, and is less willing to condemn individuals, thus tending to believe that God is available to answer prayers regardless of one's transgressions. Consequently, 20.9% of the sample viewed God as highly judgmental but not highly engaged in the world (Froese & Bader, 2010). For these individuals with a critical God-image, God's justice exists for the afterlife rather than the present world. The researchers found this type to be held most often by ethnic minorities, the poor, and the exploited (Froese & Bader, 2010). Lastly, they also found that approximately 23.9% of the sample had a distant God-image, viewing God as neither judgmental nor highly engaged with the world. In this sense, individuals view God as a cosmic force that set the laws of nature in motion but not acting upon the world or caring about human activities.

In terms of attachment to God, it was hypothesized that avoidant attachment scores would be positively correlated to all mental health outcomes. The hypothesis was partially supported. Avoidant attachment to God exhibited weak positive relationships to depression, stress, and global distress scores, and the construct was not significantly related to anxiety or worry. Increases in subjects' endorsement of attachment avoidance with God were associated with

Chapter 1: God's Compassion on Me

increases in depression, stress, and global distress scores. Attachment style to God demonstrated mixed findings with respect to religiosity. A more avoidant attachment to God was strongly associated with less endorsed religiosity, supporting the study's prediction. This follows that having the perception of an unavailable, impersonal, disinterested God may lead individuals not to see a reason to participate in a religion that is not meeting their needs.

In conclusion, the compassion of God is evident in our lives. It takes our faith to tap into His compassion and listen keenly to His voice. Like Sarah, we can get a message of consolation from our Lord, and that every manifestation is a blessing of God for us His flocks. Finding an attachment with God propels us to give thanks for His preservation, through our struggles with stress, illnesses, and pain. In meditation and prayer, you realize how much God's compassion has manifested. It cannot be that it is our own doing, but the Lord's doing. Let us share greatly in the compassion of God. Look! It lies everywhere for each of His creations.

References

-Barton, R. H. (2018). Strengthening the soul of your leadership: Seeking God in the crucible of ministry. InterVarsity Press.

-Crawford, E., Wright, M. O., & Masten, A. S. (2006). Resilience and spirituality in youth. The handbook of spiritual development in childhood and adolescence, 355-370.

-Froese, P., & Bader, C. (2010). America's Four Gods: What We Say about God--and What That Says about Us. Oxford University Press.

(To the Depressed Christian | Cru, n.d.)

(Christian Compassion and Mental Health By Zándra Bishop - CLA, n.d.)

(How Prayer Strengthens Your Emotional Health | Everyday Health, n.d.)

-Kristeller, J. L., & Johnson, T. (2005). Cultivating loving kindness: A two-stage model of the effects of meditation on empathy, compassion, and altruism. Zygon®, 40(2), 391-408.

-Leijssen, L. (2013). &apos When the Spirit of Truth Comes, He will Guide you into All the Truth. &apos (John 16: 13): Sacraments: God&aposs Revelation in Word and Spirit. Questions Liturgiques/Studies in Liturgy, 94(1), 7-26.

-Reese Masterson, A. (2013). Reproductive Health and Gender-Based Violence In Syrian Refugee Women.

Chapter 1: God's Compassion on Me

-Solmsen, F. (1964). Leisure and play in Aristotle's Ideal State. *Rheinisches Museum für Philologie, 107*(3. H), 193-220.

-Schoonover-Shoffner, K. (2016). New Year's Resolution: Be Transformed!. *Journal of Christian Nursing, 33*(1), 5.

-Tan, S. Y., & Gregg, D. H. (2010). Disciplines of the Holy Spirit: How to connect to the Spirit's power and presence. Zondervan.

About Dr. Hellen Njoroge

Dr. Hellen Njoroge is a clinical psychologist and Judicial Mediator. For over seven years, Dr Njoroge has been working with Kenya Judiciary in Alternative Dispute Reformation and as a Professional Mediator Accredited by Kenya Judiciary. Dr Njoroge is the founder of Jali Centre, a mental health organization focusing on the well-being and health of women, children, and families. Additionally, Dr. Njoroge works with survivors of Gender Based Violence, and over the last 10 years, Dr. Njoroge has served with Christ's Arms Reaching Everywhere Ministries as the Kenyan Ministry Leader. To God Be The Glory.

Chapter 1: God's Compassion on Me

God's compassion flows...

Assisting 1st year university student

Feeding the elderly

Dr. Lisa visiting Dr. Hellen at the gender violence unit
Nairobi, Kenya

Chapter 2:
Destruction of the Soul

Introduction:

This phrase is curious to many and real and alive to others. As a psychologist, the soul, will, emotions and emotional state are consistently present in my day-to-day affairs. Concern and compassion for people and for my particular clients are resident at all times. "How can you do that" you may say. How do you consistently hear the historical trauma, the abuse, neglect, sadness, torment, and so on and so forth? It's a calling and a gift God gives to some just as he anoints doctors and nurses to experience sickness, blood, and death. God equips those that he calls (*Exodus 4:10-11*). If you don't know it, God gives us just what we need, just when we need it.

Let's move on to define exactly what we are referring to with the phrase "Destruction of the Soul."

DEFINITION of the SOUL

What is the soul? Webster's New World Dictionary defines the soul as an entity that is regarded as being the immortal or spiritual part of a person and which, having no physical or material reality, is credited with the functions of thinking, willing, and choosing.

The Vine's Bible Dictionary (Strong's #5590) denotes SOUL in its various meanings and related scriptures as (a) the natural life of the body (b) the immaterial invisible part of man (Matt. 10:28) (c) The disembodied or unclothes man (d) The seat of the personality, explained as own self, (Hebrews 6:19), (e) The seat of the sentient element in man, that by he perceives, reflects, feels and desires, (Matt

God's Compassion Towards Me

11:29), (f) The seat of will and purpose, (Matt 22:37), (g) The seat of appetite. (Psalm 107:9). The spiritual, rational and immortal substance in man, which distinguishes him from brutes; that part of man which enables him to think and reason, and which renders him a subject of moral government. The immortality of the soul is a fundamental article of the Christian system. Such is the nature of the human soul that it must have a God, an object of supreme affection.

Another definition of soul is:

1. The spiritual part of a person believed to give life to the body. In religion and philosophy – the immaterial aspect or essence of a human being that confers individuality and humanity (Merriam Webster Dictionary)
2. Mind, will and emotions – the seat of the personality. (Strong's #5590)

The Vine's Expository Dictionary describes the soul as the "breath - the breath of life." The natural life of the body.

Also called the seat of the personality. In *Luke 9:25* it states – *For what is a man advantage, if he gain the whole world, and lose himself, or be cast away?*

Here is a biblical reference to what happens when we turn away from God. *Hebrews 10:39* states: *But we are not of them who draw back unto perdition; but of them that believe to the saving of the soul.* (We are the faithful ones, whose souls will be saved.)

The language of *Hebrews 4:12* states: *For the word or God is quick, and powerful, and sharper than any two-edged sword, piercing even to the dividing asunder of soul and spirit, and of the joints and marrow, and is a discerner of the thoughts and intents of the heart.* This suggests the extreme difficulty of distinguishing between the soul and the spirit, alike in their nature and

Chapter 2: Destruction of the Soul

in their activities. Generally speaking, the spirit is the higher, and the soul the lower element.

The Hebrew View of "Soul"

According to the Fellowship of Hebrew Related Ministries (FIRM) The Hebrew word for the soul is nephesh and it literally means "breath." Animals as well as human beings were created with this life breath as a gift from God. This aligns with the previously mentioned definitions of soul.

Pneuma – breath – *God breathed breath into man who was created from dust to create and Man/Soul man. (Gen 2:7)*

"Pneuma, to breathe or blow, primarily denotes the wind. Breath; the spirit which, like the wind, is invisible, immaterial, and powerful"

What's the difference between soul and spirit?

Your soul speaks of your inner-life in relation to your own experience: your mind, heart, will, and imagination. It also includes your thoughts, desires, passions, and dreams.

But your spirit speaks of the same inner life in relation to God: your faith, hope, love, character, and perseverance.

Destruction

Let's define destruction (briefly). Vine's Expository Dictionary states– to destroy, annihilate and or exterminate. The first time destruction is referred to in the bible is Gen. 34:30 which states: "I shall be destroyed." This word always expresses the act of destroying, a tearing down, a bringing to naught, subversion, demolition, ruin, slaying, devastation and the literal destruction of people.

God's Compassion Towards Me

John 10:10 states, *The thief cometh not, but for to steal, and to kill, and to destroy: I am come that they might have life, and that they might have it more abundantly.*

Ephesians 6:12 states, *For we wrestle not against flesh and blood, but against principalities, against powers, against the rulers of the darkness of this world, against spiritual wickedness in high places.*

All this indicates that the enemy is on assignment to destroy man by whatever means possible. Since we know that everything starts in the mind, will, and emotions, this is a fitting target. If the mind can be polluted by negativity and deception, the body, will, and emotions will follow.

How can the Soul be destroyed?
Man's way

Keep in mind that you have free will. God never violates a person's free will. Because people choose to do unthinkable things, because multiple spirits such as perversion, greed, and idolatry to name a few, roam the earth, people including children get hurt.

Trauma is one method the enemy uses to destroy. There are many types of trauma that people experience. Accidents, incidents, and natural disasters which are environmental.

There are other traumas that result from criminal acts such as rape, incest, molestation, and abuse. The resulting emotions often cause schisms, breaks, fissures, and cracks in the mental fiber and in the soul.

Fragmentation is another method of man-made destruction. The definition of fragmentation is when the Mind/Soul/Personality attempts to splinter into different segments to protect you. Enter multiple personalities or DID Dissociative Identity Disorder, (a label).

Chapter 2: Destruction of the Soul

Usually, one portion leads and serves as a protector to the other more vulnerable portions of the personality. This is when demonic oppression and influences can occur.

There are many different labels/diagnoses and entities. There is Depression, Anxiety, Obsessive Compulsive Disorder, Dissociative Identity Disorder, PTSD Post Traumatic Stress Disorder, ADHD Attention Deficit Hyperactivity Disorder, Bipolar Disorder (1 and 2), Borderline Personality Disorder, and a whole multitude of man-made labels. These are all open doors through which the enemy comes to torment and destroy the soul. If we revisit the pneuma (breath) and how God spoke the earth into existence, this will correspond with labeling mental health conditions as providers and people in general attempt to understand and categorize conditions. This is done in order to assist in healing the trauma, torment, pain, discomfort, and Dis-Ease.

There are chemical imbalances that can be rectified with medications. It takes a seasoned psychiatrist and therapist full of the Holy Spirit to discern the proper treatment. Enter men and women of God filled with the Holy Spirit and glory of God to be used as instruments of health and healing in multiple ways.

Many people come into therapy for the purpose of "getting themselves together." Or they may say "I had a nervous breakdown." It is true that many have had traumatic experiences, abuse, neglect, abandonment, and rejection (yes even from the womb) and as a result are experiencing many physical, emotional, and real-life disasters. People don't come to therapy without a specific problem. Some feel so hopeless and helpless as though they want to end their lives. Some people come with substance abuse from self-medicating to get away from their racing thoughts, trauma, flashbacks, and torment.

God's Compassion Towards Me

These fissures, traumas, cracks, and wounds allow the enemy to enter in and wreak havoc in the soul and spirit realm. This is how the destruction begins. People often come in with these labels, diagnoses, issues, and problems seeking shelter and relief. Let's also take into account the fact that once people are given a label, a mental illness or physical illness these are spoken to by and about them again and again. This pattern plants seeds that will grow unless they are uprooted. He also created man by breathing into the clay body He created. Isn't it ironic and predictable that the enemy would copy God and pervert His actions by using breath and words to destroy humanity?

The bottom line is that God loves everyone. Not just the saved, but the unsaved as well. He loved us so much according to *John 3:16 – For God so loved the world, that he gave his only begotten Son, that whosoever believeth in him should not perish, but have everlasting life.* It is the love of God and knowing the truth of who you are and WHOSE you are that sets people free. This is what is offered by men and women of God serving in mental health and in the marketplace. This is what sets us apart from the world and worldly methods. Can worldly systems and methodologies be successfully employed? Yes, absolutely with a generous dose of Jesus!

Segue…to the enemy's plan. Again, according to John 10:10, the enemy is out to destroy humanity. Why? Because he is jealous after being kicked out of heaven. We have taken his place to praise and worship God in all we do. The enemy's plan is primarily based on: the lust of the flesh, the lust of the eyes, and the pride of life.

These days, everyone young and old alike are inundated with stuff. Social media, TV, movies, drugs, alcohol, fame, fortune, and so on and so forth. On social media, everything and everyone appears to be perfect, successful, rich, happy, and well-balanced. People APPEAR to have everything they want or need. The key emphasis here is how

Chapter 2: Destruction of the Soul

things appear. Enter the enemy once again, bringing deception and delusions. This causes people to envy, covet and try to imitate what is most likely fraud, deception, or delusion. Enter the Lust of the Flesh and the Lust of the Eyes. We want what we can't have. It seems right. In *Proverbs 14:12* it says: *There is a way which seemeth right unto a man, But the end thereof are the ways of death.*

The Enemy's Way
What is the Lust of the flesh?

It's based on envy and covetousness. What is envy? Envy is wanting what we don't have. We can often idolize what we see other's having. The enemy often tag teams us with the Lust of the flesh and the Lust of the eyes. Both of these things cause us to take our eyes off God and fall to what the world sees as successful and rich – the ultimate achievement in life. Money, power, influence, stuff. But... once achieved, the God spot in our souls is still left empty and the soul is being eaten away by what the flesh and mind drive toward in performance-based thinking. If we could just get one more thing, one more dollar, one more job, the wife, the husband, the car, the house, the position, the following which is all idol worship.

What is the lust of the eyes?

The lust of the eyes causes us to want what we don't have because it looks good, and desirable and will possibly make us look and feel successful. The lust of the eyes and flesh involves how people look and feel. Do women have the perfect hourglass figure? People are paying to be made perfect and often dying in the process from mommy makeovers to Brazilian butt lifts to leaking implants. The most beautiful hair and skin devoid of wrinkles or imperfections are preferable. **Let's just note that only Jesus is perfect.** Do men have the perfect physique, perfect performance, and beautiful skin and hair

– beards and hair transplants, penile enhancements, and bodybuilding fraught with steroids? All these things destroy the soul, the mind, and the thinking patterns of people. It is idolatry at its finest. Often times this covetousness causes mental torment in trying to be perfect. It opens the door to the enemy who attacks the nervous system, our OS (operating system) the brain. It opens the door for the demons of depression, oppression, anxiety, fear, lack, bipolar, schizophrenia, and more as the splintering of the soul occurs. This double-mindedness and disassociation often brings folks running for help. The book of James 1:6-8 talks of being unstable (double-minded). *James 1:6 –But let him ask in faith, nothing wavering. For he that waveth is like a wave of the sea driven with the wind and tossed.* It is the turning away of people from Christ and his perfect creation which is YOU!

What is the Pride of life?

The pride of life is another destructive force. What is the definition of pride? According to the Oxford Language Dictionary, it is a feeling of deep pleasure or satisfaction derived from one's own achievements, the achievements of those with whom one is closely associated, or from qualities or possessions that are widely admired. People mistakenly feel they have it all together until their life topples much like the tower of Babel. Be mindful that this is why satan was kicked out of heaven. This destroys the soul. It turns people away from God and it distorts and derails, aims their focus toward themselves. What does God say about pride? Proverbs 8:13 states, *The fear of the Lord is to hate evil: Pride, and arrogancy, and the evil way, And the froward mouth, do I hate.* And finally, Proverbs 16:5 states, *Every one that is proud in heart is an abomination to the LORD.*

Offense ties in with all of the above destructive methods. Offense according to Merriam Webster is something that causes a person to be hurt, angry or upset; something that is wrong or improper or a criminal

Chapter 2: Destruction of the Soul

act. When we become offended it opens the door to the enemy. A door for torment, abandonment, rejection, anger, frustration, and revenge. When we become and continue to be offended the enemy has succeeded in driving a wedge between us and God. Resentment and anger allow a root of bitterness and the accompanying spirits to build a stronghold (impenetrable fortress) in a person's soul, will, and emotions. This is a destructive force to be reckoned with.

Many of the above destructive forces have a rider attached or a 'ride-along'. It's called AOD or alcohol and other drugs. This is a trap many fall into to escape unmet needs, unmet expectations, disappointments, trauma, and a host of other events that have befallen them in life. Having no coping skills and often no one to walk through it with them, they choose to escape from the things the enemy is consistently throwing at their minds with his fiery darts (memories, trauma, abuse, disappointment, FEAR, jealousy, and more). Drugs/pharmacopeia can be used in the hand of professionals as a means for treating physical and mental health diseases. The enemy steps in and perverts the usage causing people to become hooked and dependent on these things rather than God. Destruction follows.

There is Help

This help is God's Redemptive plan for humanity, for society for YOU!!! Jesus paid the price and carried all our afflictions of the mind, soul, and spirit as well as any infirmity we might have to the cross. It's a done deal and has been paid in FULL. So… you may say, how do we realize and experience this freedom? I'm glad you asked.

As servants of God in our various titles from Psychiatrists to Counselors to Therapists to Psychologists, we have been commissioned by God to bring about healing from mental torment. This is what we have been designed for and we need the Holy Spirit's assistance in everything we think, say, and do. Without Holy Spirit, we can use book knowledge and experience, but we need the secrets of God to expedite the healing once and for all. I am glad to be of use as a vessel to help bring healing to people of every race, culture, creed, age, and persuasion.

Inner Healing and Deliverance

One of the ways I help people to recover is through inner healing. This is a method that is prescribed in biblical terms. In John 8:32 it says, *and ye shall know the truth, and the truth shall make you free.* Inner healing takes specific memories, identified by the person and walks through them. While doing so, the lie the enemy has planted in their mind, soul, and emotions is identified. We invite Jesus/Holy Spirit into the memory to show them the truth of how they are seen by God and that they belong to Him. In so doing, people are set free from patterns of behavior, false beliefs, and torment such as depression, anxiety, fear, abandonment, rejection, and other things. In knowing the truth, they are set free and no longer experience the lie. Lie-based thinking and fear are often the root cause of many mental health conditions. Using inner healing through the Holy Spirit, love, and other principles is what allows Christian mental health practitioners to make a lasting difference in healing. There are other ministry tools and programs such as Sozo, Deliverance, and Reconciliation Ministries to name a few that are used in a different domain.

Forgiveness

To slam the door in the enemy's face we must forgive. Forgive yourself and forgive others. Forgive for yourself, not for others. This is in no way allowing the other person off the hook. It instead empowers God to work on you and them. Forgiveness is essential in this journey to wellness. The recommendation is to forgive them, release them and

Chapter 2: Destruction of the Soul

bless them. The Bible states in Matthew 6:14 it states: *For if ye forgive men their trespasses, your heavenly Father will also forgive you:*

I hope this has illuminated the fight being fought in the spirit and in the earth realm for your soul. We as health care practitioners stand with and for you to WIN in every situation and walk in the freedom that Jesus Christ has promised you through His redemptive plan.

SHALOM and blessings unto you.

About Dr. Lisa G. Brooks

Dr. Lisa G. Brooks was born and raised in Ann Arbor, Michigan. Dr. Brooks is the mother of 2 adult sons and 6 grandchildren. Dr. Brooks began writing in high school for therapeutic purposes. Dr. Lisa G. Brooks has been counseling since 2000. She received her BA from Michigan State University, MS in Behavior Psychology from Eastern Michigan University, and a Doctorate in Ministry from Destiny Christian University. Dr. Brooks is the author of *Defeating the New Pandemic: Offense – Defense: Who Wins?* and has taught at the Community College level and in the College domain. She has worked in corporate America and in corrections. She has also had the pleasure of facilitating multiple workshops and trainings. Dr. Brooks is a Limited License Psychologist who is licensed by the State of Michigan and has CAADC (Certified Advanced Alcohol and Drug Addiction Counselor) credentials in the State of Michigan and Georgia.

Book by Dr. Lisa G. Brooks

Defeating The NEW PANDEMIC is all about overcoming and defeating offense and other strongholds that attempt to steal our joy and freedom in Christ.

ISBN 13: 979-8364659859

$15.00

Chapter 3:
Inner Turmoil

"Come to me, all you who are weary and burdened, and I will give you rest. Take my yoke upon you and learn from me, for I am gentle and humble in heart, and you will find rest for your souls." -Matthew 11:28-29

At some point or another, all human beings experience emotional suffering. That suffering becomes a threat to personal well-being when we are unable to recognize the existence of internal conflict within ourselves (Michaelson, 2020). When the internal conflict is left unresolved, discord occurs which instigates irritability, hostility, defensiveness, and hopelessness (Michaelson, 2020). These dynamics are attributes of inner turmoil. Although most of our suffering is avoidable (Michaelson, 2020), oftentimes we exacerbate agony and blindly impede human progress instead of trusting in our faith in God and falling back on the support of our family and friends.

My Road to Inner Turmoil

Almost two years ago, I began my doctoral studies in clinical psychology. As I had expected, things started off smoothly. I was absorbing the new knowledge like a sponge and managing the expectations and responsibilities of being a doctoral student. I immersed myself in research projects, student organizations, and national organizations. I managed my time well and maintained a school-life balance by prioritizing time with my husband and daughter. Fast forward to several months ago when it seems everything began falling apart. I had taken on so many roles and responsibilities that there was no time to sleep, let alone enjoy my time. Each night, I

God's Compassion Towards Me

stayed up until 4 am or 5 am, which was followed by my alarm sounding at 6 am alerting me to get myself and my daughter ready for the day. I barely ate – I did not have time to eat, but most distressing was the weekly traumatization I experienced in my multicultural psychology course each Wednesday.

As a Black woman, I have spent most of my life codeswitching and making myself small to fit into White spaces, however, I could not bear that weight during my multicultural class. As I reflect on my experiences with the course content, my classmates' responses and reactions, and the assignments, my mind and body have become filled with anxiety and grief; I am *triggered*. I was triggered sitting in class each week and I am triggered now. When I say "triggered," I am referring to this visceral reaction I feel inside my entire body. I want to vomit to stop the gnawing and aching in my stomach. I feel piercing tension in my neck and back. My head aches. I am triggered.

If you were to ask me to pinpoint a specific part of the course that was triggering, I could not. On the first day of class, we were shown a video with graphic footage of Black women being brutalized by the police. I had seen the video before, but as a Black woman, the impact never lessens. During a subsequent class, we were shown a video in which Native American, Dr. Fish, described her experiences of being an Indigenous child in a predominately white school. She explained how her experiences led her to create a new version of Bronfenbrenner's Ecological model in which historical factors are centered in the chronosystem as opposed to the individual (Fish & Syed, 2018). Her (his)story resonated with me given the fact that my experiences in predominately white academic settings have been riddled with exclusion, oppression, ostracism, and racism. Hearing her speak was *triggering*. It brought up memories of being told, "I can't play with you, because you're Black" and "You fell down the toilet and that's why your skin is dark." It brought up feelings of not being good

Chapter 3: Inner Turmoil

enough, feelings of worthlessness, and hatred of my Blackness. That was the beginning of my inner turmoil.

I was regularly forced to face the reality that my race and skin color, the most inescapable part of myself, would always make me less than others. I became consumed with those thoughts. The only way to prove that I was not less than my White counterparts, was to work even harder. I was obsessed with proving my worth; my intelligence; my right to just exist.

My trials and tribulations did not stop there. During my most recent semester in school, it felt like I was getting hit with brick after brick. I experienced multiple microaggressions from my cohort members and faculty. I was ignored and gaslit by my primary care physician. As a result, I was hospitalized for my physical health. This led to temporary cognitive decline and impacted my productivity. I had never felt so powerless, and I began having frequent panic attacks.

I often found myself questioning why I was so hellbent on earning my doctorate degree. I kept asking myself if it would be worth all the strife and pain in the end. I was being tormented daily in every aspect of my life. My physical health and my psychological well-being were continuously being placed at risk. Even still, I never gave up.

I can recall the day after I came home from the hospital sitting at my kitchen table with my husband and mother-in-law. I was reflecting on a clinical training meeting that had occurred the day before going to the emergency room. During this meeting, I learned that most accredited internship sites for my program have minimum clinical training hours in specific psychological areas. The tragedy of receiving this information was the timing of it. Dwelling on that knowledge triggered a panic attack.

From the moment I entered my doctorate program, I have positioned myself to have limitless options for my internship and future career. After attending that meeting, all my hard work and accomplishments felt minute. I realized that my internship options are limited because I was not provided the needed information prior to choosing my current practicum site. That is when the inner turmoil really set in.

I sat at the table hyperventilating and hysterically crying. I screamed, "Why?" "What have I been working so hard for?" "What have all of these sacrifices been for?" "I have done everything right." I have been working ten times harder than everyone else and missing out on my daughter's childhood." I struggled to catch my breath. My head was pounding. I was defeated. I lost my motivation to keep pushing forward. I felt hopeless. I felt helpless. I was extremely sad and irritable. I constantly dwelled and ruminated on everything that was going wrong. It felt as though everything in my life was out of my control. My troubled thoughts were in the driver's seat, and they kept playing their sadistic messages on repeat. Then, finally, one day I had enough.

Overcoming My Inner Turmoil

It was an ordinary morning filled with stress, anxiety, grief, and turmoil, but this day I could not take it anymore. I was sitting in church listening to a guest pastor preach about fighting. He talked about our need to fight against racism. He said we need to fight against poverty. He said we need to fight against the devil. As I began sobbing, I surrendered to God. I begged and pleaded. My bones felt so heavy. I told God that I could not carry the weight anymore. I told him that I did not have any fight left in me – that I had been fighting every day of my life. I told him that this fight was His now. I laid it all on the table.

The next day, I woke up feeling burdenless. God had taken the weight from my shoulders. I was ready to pick up my sword and keep fighting – not out of a sense of obligation, but because it is what I have

Chapter 3: Inner Turmoil

been called to do. I began relying on my faith. I began thinking positively. I began prioritizing my mental and physical health. I started seeing drastic changes in my mood, motivation, and overall well-being.

A Way Out for Anyone

My story is one of many like it. Human beings often experience life stressors, and it is not uncommon for inner turmoil to take hold and their lives to unravel. The good news is that inner turmoil can be conquered by developing an understanding of the self as a relationship (Redekop, 2014) and using that knowledge to facilitate and strengthen relationships with God, family, and friends.

Inner turmoil, or being in conflict with oneself (Seltzer, 2015), can present itself differently in different people. Agitation, confusion, self-torturing, ruminating, hopelessness, tension, overwhelmingness, fear, powerlessness, and indecisiveness are all characteristics of inner turmoil (Seltzer, 2015). No matter the individual or the specific features that are present, one thing is for certain, which is that leaning on faith can help transcend inner conflict and stressful times (Goodman, 2020). In times of adversity, relationships with God can promote healing and provide opportunities for growth. Through prayer, one can foster a sense of connectedness and seek ways to improve one's life. This is especially important because our faith and connection to God can cultivate empowerment and hope.

In addition to our relationships with God, our support from family can be an integral part of moving through and out of inner turmoil. Quality family support is associated with decreased mental distress and increased perceptions of health (Cano et al., 2003). Family support also plays a critical role in promoting healing, lowering suffering, and preventing sustained anguish (Aass, 2021). Falling back on familial support in times of distress can mediate positive emotions and increase overall well-being through connection.

Similar to familial support, connections with friends can be crucial to tackling inner turmoil. Time spent with friends produces countless long-term physical, emotional, and mental health benefits (Lawler, 2021). Friendships can help increase one's sense of belonging, improve self-worth, and help reduce stress (Mayo Clinic Staff, 2012). These factors are all significant influences in working through inner turmoil. Furthermore, maintaining and nurturing healthy friendships foster enriched lives (Mayo Clinic Staff, 2012), which decreases the impact and severity of inner turmoil.

Summary

A natural part of being a human being in this world is experiencing suffering and turmoil (Pillay, 2020). When life gets difficult or times get hard, it is normal to feel emotions such as irritability, stress, or helplessness. When such emotions become overwhelming and an individual becomes consumed with their inner conflict and negative thoughts, calling on family and turning to friends can improve mental health and well-being while decreasing distress. Most importantly, one's connection with and faith in God can be a source of solace and refuge.

References

Aass, L. K., Moen, O. L., Skundberg-Kletthagen, H., Lundqvist, L., & Schroder, A. (2021). Family support and quality of community mental health care: Perspectives from families living with mental illness. *Journal of Clinical Nursing, 31*(7-8), 935-948. https://doi.org/10.1111/jocn.15948

Cano, A., Scaturo, D. J., Sprafkin, R. P., Lantinga, L. J., Fiese, B. H., & Brand, F. (2003). Family support, self-rated health, and psychological distress. *Primary Care Companion to the Journal of Clinical Psychiatry, 5*(3), 111-117. https://doi.org/10.4088pcc.v05n0302

Fish, J. & Syed, M. (2018). Native Americans in higher education: An ecological systems perspective. *Journal of College Student Development, 59*(4), 387-403. https://doi.org/10.1353/csd.2018.0038

Goodman, B. (2020). *Faith in a time of crisis.* American Psychological Association. Retrieved from https://www.apa.org/topics/covid-19/faith-crisis

Lawler, M. (2021). Why friendships are so important for health and well-being. *Everyday Health.* Retrieved from https://www.everydayhealth.com/emotional-health/social-support.aspx

Mayo Clinic Staff (2012). Friendships: Enrich your life and improve your health. *Mayo Clinic.* Retrieved from https://www.mayoclinic.org/healthy-lifestyle/adult-health/in-depth/friendships/art-20044860

Michaelson, P. (2020). The hazards of inner conflict. *Transformative insights from depth psychology.* Retrieved from https://whywesuffer.com/inner-conflict-primt-instigator-of-our-dysfunction/

Seltzer, L. F. (2015). *What causes your inner turmoil? When you're at war with yourself, there's generally a good reason.* Sussex Publishers, LLC. Retrieved from https://www.psychologytoday.com/au/blog/evolution-of-the-self/201504/what-causes-you-inner-turmoil

Redekop, P. (2014). Inner peace and conflict transformation. *Peace Research: The Canadian Journal of Peace and Conflict Studies, 46*(2), 31-49. https://www.jstor.org/stable/24896064

About Doctoral Candidate Courtney Cabell

Doctoral Candidate Courtney Cabell is a licensed psychotherapist in the state of Michigan where she practices from a Humanistic and Black feminist lens. She earned her BA in psychology from the University of Michigan – Ann Arbor (2016), her MS in psychology from Southern New Hampshire University (2020), and her MA in clinical psychology from the Michigan School of Psychology (MSP) (2021).

Currently, Candidate Cabell is a second-year doctoral student at MSP where she serves as a student ambassador, a student representative for the Institutional Equity Anti-Racism Committee, the secretary for the Inclusion, Diversity, and Equity Alliance, and president of the Psi Chi chapter. She is also the founder and president of the Association of Black Psychologists Student Circle Chapter at MSP. Courtney serves as the Junior Student Representative for APA's Division 32, Society for Humanistic Psychology, and as the Vice Chair of the Michigan Psychological Association's Graduate Students (MPAGS).

Mrs. Cabell has a passion for serving marginalized and minoritized populations, with a specific interest in trauma. These passions and interests led her to found Open Heart Communities, a non-profit organization of which she is the active CEO, whose mission is serving foster children and youth who have aged out of foster care.

To contact Courtney Cabell:
www.courtneycabell.com | cabellwellness@gmail.com

Chapter 4:
Not Good Enough

It appears since COVID, I have recognized we as women tend to not feel good about ourselves more so than men. While both men and women battle with insecurities, one may wonder, how is it that a person may not feel good enough. I pray as you read this chapter, it will begin to resonate in your mind, hearts, and spirit that you are good enough because God created you. A popular saying is that God will take the ordinary and make it extraordinary. We must know and remember wherever we may start, God will continue to equip us with everything we need.

In 2009, my former church hosted our first Women's ministry. A friend of one of our guest speakers had flown in from California to support this great woman of God. At the end of the service, she asked if she could give me a Word she believed God was giving her for me. Being a member of a prophetic church, I was open to hearing what she believed God was telling her for me. To my surprise, a part of the Word was that I would be writing manuscripts. I must share that this surprised me as I had not thought, desired, or had any intention of writing anything. At that time, I had no idea that I would be furthering my education. So here today, I sit writing…Praise God!

When Dr. Lisa H. Fuller approached me, I could not help but to laugh as I remembered that Word. The scripture that comes to my mind is Isaiah 55:11 which reads *"So shall my word be that goeth forth out of my mouth: it shall not return unto me void, but it shall accomplish that which I please, and it shall prosper in the thing whereto I sent it."* I pray that as you read this chapter, it ministers and encourages you that God will back His word concerning you. You are good enough, take those thoughts captive (II Corinthians 10:5), and do not let fear of any kind or people stop you.

As I prepared to write this chapter, I realized I did not experience any fear in writing as a contributing author, so I encourage you to move beyond any fear. It could be fear of man, fear of what people may think or feel about what God has called you to do, fear of failure, and even fear of success. Move beyond the fear and the anxiety.

Where Does it All Begin?

I believe that many times when we experience insecurities about ourselves, we may not necessarily know where they stem from. Personally, I did not realize that I was experiencing feeling not good enough and comparing myself to others. While I knew that I was capable of doing more or doing better, I suffered from low self-esteem in certain areas, a lack of confidence, and self-doubt. I always had a good job, took college classes which lead to obtaining three degrees, and served in ministry, yet I was still lacking. I have had wonderful mentors, most of whom were very encouraging and supportive of my endeavors. There were times I would be prayed for or given a prophetic word and the matter of self-esteem, confidence, and doubting myself would be included. My thought at times would be, well, I am doing this, I am doing that, so why am I hearing about having insecurities? I began to ponder over this so that I could understand.

In September 2018, I attended a seminar at my church for inner healing and deliverance. While inner healing and deliverance were not new to me, the method in which these were facilitated gave me a better understanding of how it can be done to be more effective for a person. Without giving every detail of the process, during this time I was in the doctoral program at Destiny School of Ministry. While doing my dissertation, I highlighted the importance of inner healing and

Chapter 4: Not Good Enough

deliverance as one of the chapters to encourage those in ministry to consider allowing them to be more effective as a servant of God. Unbeknownst to me, this chapter allowed me to not only reflect, but I experienced a revelation that I did not recall earlier from when I was a little girl.

I grew up on the east side of Detroit on Lenox Street. My grandparents helped in raising me. As I was reflecting, I began to think back to the days when I would be on Lenox visiting and my birth father's best friend lived a few doors down the street. It was usually my great-grandmother or my grandmother who would see him on his best friend's porch. My great-grandmother would tell me "Your dad is down the street, go say hi and ask him for some ice cream money." Back then, ice cream was less than a dollar off the ice cream truck. In my excitement of knowing that my "dad" was down the street, I would run outside and down the street to see him, say hi, and ask for ice cream money. He would see me running towards him and he would literally end his visit with his best friend to jump in his car and drive off. I did not understand. When coming back to the house, I did not know how to explain that I did not get my ice cream money. Eventually, it had come to a point that when I saw my birth father at his friend's house, I would turn back around to keep him from seeing me. I would retreat to our backyard or at least to where I would not be seen between the houses.

I am not sure how long before I learned to not have any expectations in seeing my birth father or getting any money for ice cream, but I believe this is when I learned not to have any expectations of my father or anyone. I share this because this was added rejection and abandonment for me. I did not know what it was to have a father, a daddy that loved you and thought of you as his little girl to protect and teach things that a daughter should know. I share this because I believe that because of this experience, I did not know how to look at

God's Compassion Towards Me

God as my daddy or as my father. I went through life experiencing things that could have possibly been avoided when dating. This is a sidebar and perhaps for another book, but for the ladies, when dating or desiring a husband, you can inadvertently date men with traits of your father. I understand why children are upset about not having their fathers. It is something about having that love, encouragement, protection, guidance, and support that only a father can give to help you to grow and have that self-esteem and confidence.

Life Experiences

I recall being a part of or in proximity of conversations held by older adult women sharing their thoughts, views, and opinions related to young mothers, teenage mothers in particular, and children born out of wedlock. I initially found myself fearful of sharing that I was one of those children. There were negative perceptions towards teen mothers and the potential outcomes of babies born to teenage moms. I would at times quietly wonder what these women would think of me if I shared that my mom was a teen mom. It took many years for me to be able to share this and not be fearful or embarrassed by what someone may have thought. What we must remember is that people's opinions about us do not matter, it only matters what God thinks of us. This is an example for me as to how your environment can affect or impact how you think. What's amazing is that today, I am an example of what you can become despite what a person's perception may be. When you have a good support system and determination, you can do anything that you put your mind to. I cannot guarantee that it will be easy, but we know the scripture, Philippians 4:13 "I can do all things through Christ which strengtheneth me."

Chapter 4: Not Good Enough

What Are You Speaking?

"The power of the spoken word is one of life's greatest mysteries. All you will ever be or accomplish hinges on how you choose to govern what comes out of your mouth."
Cindy Trimm

Proverbs 18:21 is a very familiar passage that is quoted *"Death and life are in the power of the tongue: and they that love it shall eat the fruit thereof."* We will have what we say when we speak. Our words are powerful and will impact every area of our lives. Words have so much power over our minds and there can be casualties when we say what we think. What comes to mind is that I remember recently watching a program where there were two plants encased in either glass or plastic. The two plants were in a school and the children were assigned the task of speaking positive words to one plant and negative words to the other. I do not remember how long this project ran for, but literally, the one plant that was spoken to with negative words began to fade in the color of yellow and brown, and this plant began to bend over to one side. The plant that had positive words spoken to it was standing strong and appeared to have grown taller, it was beautiful in color and full of life.

Our words can build, limp, and even tear down. Our lives, thoughts, and emotions will go in the direction of our tongues by what we speak. The scripture that comes to mind is James 3:4. *"Behold also the ships, which though they be so great, and are driven of fierce winds, yet are they turned about with a very small helm, withersoever the governor listeth."* If you have seen the bottom of a ship, that rudder is small, yet has the ability to turn a ship, boat, submarine, and other vehicles through the air or water. The rudder is referred to as a primary control. Just imagine having those moments of low self-esteem, self-doubt, and not feeling that you are good enough, when you begin to speak the right words to build and encourage yourself or others, what do you see? You see yourself as strong, growing, and doing the impossible. You will begin to run toward the challenges and not away from them. You can have the life you want. I get it, many times we may feel stuck, but until we start speaking, believing, and thinking the right things, things, there will be no movement or change. It may be immediate, or it may take some time, but you can arrive at your destination.

When I am counseling or coaching clients, there are times when they desire immediate results. A word I will share when they may be in a tough place, I remind them that the problem or challenge that they are facing did not happen overnight, it took some time to get there. I encourage them to set a goal or plan to focus on so that they may arrive at the positive places they want to be. This will entail having a written plan, speaking positive words, and keeping your thoughts pure and focused, including watching your circles of influence. Sometimes we must keep quiet in our family and friend groups while still speaking about those good things we desire. You are good enough to have your heart's desires, but what are you speaking?

The Comparison Trap

We have to become okay with starting where we are no matter what the endeavor. With so much being in social media today, it can be quite easy to fall into the comparison trap and limit ourselves because of what we see or think. There are numerous ideas that I have had and have come across other women who are working on my idea. Have I been hesitant to move forward because of what I see? Absolutely! But does this mean that I will not move forward? Absolutely not! I have to trust that God will continue to direct me and have the right people to support me. Better yet, I will be a solution to their problem.

When we have ideas, we must trust what we feel and believe on the inside. Our idea, plan, or vision could be perfected so that it's a million-dollar idea. I am not promising financial gain for every idea, but releasing that idea, plan, or vision on the inside can bless others and we have a return on that investment put out I recalled someone recently

Chapter 4: Not Good Enough

sharing with me that social media can be frustrating for some. A person can have the right manuscript, right lighting, dress, marketing, and other things that will be appealing to have a following, but this person may not have started at the top. I encourage every person reading this to start where you are. Do not look at where others are in their journey whether it be spiritually, professionally, in personal life, in business or in other areas. Zechariah 4:10 comes to mind at the beginning of the scripture, *For who hath despised the day of small things?* This scripture is pertaining to Zerubbabel in the rebuilding of the temple. But as it applies to us today, laying foundations can be tedious work and create discomfort, but watching what you put your hands to grow can and will be amazing; especially when we have the backing of God or under the direction of God. This goes for any area in life.

Starting small is not a bad thing. Should there be setbacks, disappointments, and failures, it's okay. You might ask, "Why is it okay?" It's an opportunity to build resilience. When we face life challenges building character, resilience, and management of our emotions will be key. All of this means knowing that you are good enough, you are going to grow in confidence, self-esteem, and belief in yourself.

It is stated that it's human nature to measure prosperity or success against neighbors, friends, co-workers, and society overall. When you think of one of the Ten Commandments is "do not covet" what others have. Comparing yourself to someone else further increases the feelings of not being enough, self-doubt, and insecurities. The person that you should be in competition with is your best self. Compete with you and win!

God's Compassion Towards Me

What Does God's Word Say

Psalm 139:13-14 – *For thou has possessed my reins: thou hast covered me in my mother's womb. I will praise thee; for I am fearfully and wonderfully made: marvellous are thy works are they works; and that my soul knoweth right well.*

Matthew 10:30-31 – *But the very hairs of your head are numbered. Fear ye not therefore, ye are of more value than many sparrows.*

Philippians 1:6 – *Being confident of this very thing, that he which hath begun a good work in you will perform it until the day of Jesus Christ.*

I Peter 2:9 – *But ye are a chosen generation, a royal priesthood, an holy nation a peculiar people; that ye should show forth the praises of him who hath called you out of darkness into his marvellous light;*

Hebrews 12:2 – *Looking unto Jesus the author and finisher of our faith; who for the joy that was set before us him endured the cross, despising the shame, and is set down at the right hand of the throne of God.*

Luke 1:37 – *For with God nothing shall be impossible.*

I Corinthians 3:16 – *Know ye that ye are the temple of God, and that the Spirit of God dwelleth in you?*

II Timothy 1:7 – *For God hath not given us the spirit of fear; but of power, and of love, and of a sound mind.*

II Corinthians 5:17 – *Therefore if any man be in Christ, he is a new creature: old things are passed away; behold all things are become new.*

Isaiah 64:8 – *But now, O Lord, thou art our father; we are the clay, and thou our potter; and we all are the work of thy hand.*

Philippians 4:13 – *I can do all things through Christ which strengtheneth me.*

Romans 12:2 – *And be not conformed to this world: but be ye transformed by the renewing of your mind, that ye may prove what is that good, and acceptable, and perfect will of God.*

Chapter 4: Not Good Enough

Jeremiah 29:11 – *For I know the thoughts that I think toward you, saith the Lord, thoughts of peace, and not of evil, to give you an expected end.*

There are additional scriptures we can reference when we begin to battle with not feeling good enough, unworthy, or self-doubt. But God our Father, Abba Father, Who is in heaven loves us so much! If only we knew how much our heavenly Father loves us. If we could only imagine seeing God's love for us, we would know we could do anything. Picture yourself laying or sitting at the feet of Jesus, or with your head in His lap telling Him all about your insecurities, your fears and doubt. Imagine being told how wonderful you are, how strong you are, how beautiful you are. See this is what a daddy does. He lets you know you are His and you can do anything. We are children of the Most High King, daughters and sons, everything we need is within us, we just have to learn how to walk through this journey. Another scripture that comes to mind is Psalm 46:5 – *God is in the midst of her; she shall not be moved: God shall help her, and that right early.* We must remind ourselves of not only who we are, but whose we are.

One of the best examples shared with me to consider when we think of who God is to us is thinking of the role of parents. Whether you were raised in a household with one parent, two parents, or the person(s) responsible for your upbringing, think of the guidance, support, and love that was given. Many times, we battle with not feeling good enough due to unwise choices, rebellion, being that wild child, bad decisions, or being influenced by the wrong person. No matter what the situation was, as any good parent would, God loves us no matter what.

Life will come with unpleasant or undesired experiences, but we have to know God is with us through all our trials, new opportunities, ministry, marriages, and business endeavors. God is there and we are good enough to fulfill the promises he has bestowed upon us.

God's Compassion Towards Me

When I think about where I currently hold many capacities, there were times whereby I questioned if this is where God wanted me. Even as a minister and entrepreneur, I had moments whereby I thought about not moving forward with a plan because I was looking at where other ladies were in life. We should not compare ourselves to others. No, we are not going to know everything or even have all the answers all the time, but we can start with what we know and build from there. Philippians 4:13 says, *"I can do all things through Christ which strengtheneth me."* Even when first coming to Christ we take baby steps. We all know when babies first learn to walk, they may stumble, trip, and fall. But babies get back up again and will either start where they have fallen or crawl to a new spot to get back up again. They may pull up with the assistance of a couch, chair, or something sturdy that they can balance themselves on. This is what we are to do, get back up again when we stumble. I am not speaking of sin per se, but accomplishing those things that God has for us. Being a Christian serving people in mental health, this may require creative ways in applying godly principles to help others who may struggle when feeling not good enough.

Steps to Overcome

1. Acknowledge – Face your feelings.
2. Select someone who is a trusted and godly vessel who will be a person of positive support.
3. Spend time in prayer and fasting writing your goals or making a vision board to guide you in your endeavors.
4. Start where you are, do NOT compare yourself to others. Remind yourself of what you have achieved.
5. Focus on the process and not the results. Be careful not to rely on the expectations of people.
6. Remember to be grateful, thankful and to look on the bright side. Your future is bright!

Chapter 4: Not Good Enough

7. Celebrate you!

Words of Encouragement for You

As I close this chapter, there is a song that I encourage you to listen to. The song is *You Say* by Lauren Daigle. This song was introduced during one of our Women's Ministry sessions. As I was praying over what should be included, this song came to my mind. I had forgotten until working on my chapter today and this song appeared on YouTube during a break I was taking. There are 11 scriptures you may reference reminding you of what God's Word says about you. I pray that this chapter ministers to you.

To everyone reading this chapter, you were created for purpose. You are a solution to someone's problem. Your presence and your ability to influence can make a difference. Remember you are good enough because you are a daughter or son of the King. There will be high and lows in life but keep taking each step forward as you discover who you are and reach the destiny God has for you (Jeremiah 29:11).

Cited Works

www.KingJamesbibleonline.com

Thomas Nelson, Inc. The Holy Bible, King James Version. Nashville, TN: Thomas Nelson Publishers, 1989.

Trimm, Cindy, Unstoppable: Compete with your best self and win. Stockbridge, GA: N. Cindy Trimm, LLC, 2021

Vaughn, Alaine Victoria, Face your Pharoah. Bloomington, IN: Westbow Press, 2021.

https://womenlivingwell.org/2021/10/10-verses-for-when-you-feel-like-you-are-not-good-enough

Chapter 4: Not Good Enough

About Dr. Bronwyn M. Davis

Bronwyn M. Davis is a Master's prepared Licensed Professional Counselor (LPC-NCC), Certified Coach (Mental Health, Lifestyle & Wellness), speaker, instructor, etiquette consultant, mentor, contributing author (God's Compassion on Me) and a Licensed minister of the Gospel. Bronwyn also obtained a Doctorate in Religious Education from Destiny School of Ministry in 2020 and teaches at Destiny for the Christian Counseling Institute. Bronwyn is founder/CEO and Clinic Director of A Safe Place Clinical Counseling, PLLC in Michigan along with two other businesses in the areas of coaching and women's wellness. Bronwyn is a member of Evangel Christian Church in Roseville, MI. As a counselor, Bronwyn possesses a genuine interest in others, an ability to listen, and a desire to see others healed, empowered, and succeeding in life.

To contact Dr. Davis:
313-365-0456 | ASafePlacePLLC@gmail.com

Chapter 5:
It's Never Too Late

What is Domestic Violence?

Violence has become widespread in American society. Every day people are writing or talking (talk shows, books, magazines, and news media) about domestic violence. Many definitions are given to describe the source, meaning, and solutions to domestic violence. According to *The Chicago Metropolitan Battered Women's Network,* domestic violence is described as: "Spouse abuse, partner violence, intimate partner violence, battering, and numerous other terms. It is a pattern of coercion used by one person to exert power and control over another person in the context of a dating, family, or household relationship". Violence generates fear in the lives of domestic violence victims. Women live in fear for their lives and the lives of their children. These women fear the possibility of another assault on themselves or their children. A longitudinal narrative (historical story) analysis of ten sheltered women, differentiated several successive stages of fear: Extreme undifferentiated fear (general fearfulness with no target); specific fear of the male partner; and lesser, chronic background fear or an ambiance of fear.

The Dynamics of Domestic Violence

As stated before, the overall aim of the abuser is to assert power and maintain control. Most relationships are not violent when they begin, but as the perpetrator gains more control over the victim, the violence escalates. Physical violence is often cyclical and recurrent. "Most survivors of domestic violence may not look battered" or may not be able to discuss their abusive relationships due to emotional wounding. The following are descriptions of types of abuse:

Physical abuse can be described as "spitting, scratching, biting, hair pulling, shaking, shoving, pushing, throwing, twisting, slapping, punching, choking, strangling, burning and the use of weapons." Physical abuse can reoccur and escalates in how many times it happens and how severe the abuse becomes for the victim. It may begin with a verbal put down, then a slap to the arm, then a slap to the face, and then a punch or kick to the body. It can escalate even to the point of death for the victim. Physical abuse involves any aspect of harm to the physical body.

Sexual abuse can be described as using physical force, which may "include rape, being forced to watch pornography or even coerced to participate in pornography." When sexual abuse occurs in relationships, it is often difficult for women to discuss and disclose. It may also refer to intimidating the victim to engage in sexual activity that is unsafe and demeaning, resulting in the victim feeling helpless and hopeless. This form of abuse may leave her feeling like a sexual object and often reduces her worth and dignity.

Emotional/psychological abuse is "much more difficult to recognize and recover from. It involves controlling the victim through fear and degradation." Emotional/psychological abuse is also described as a means to destroy the victim's sense and freedom of who she is. It is described as using words or other intimidating expressions to blame, demean, or belittle the character and confidence of the victim. When this tactic is completed by the perpetrator, the victim's life is under the rule of a dictator and is easily controlled. The victim is being told what to do, what to wear, whom she is allowed to talk to, whether or not to leave the house, or even to participate in minor chores such as watering

Chapter 5: It's Never Too Late

or cutting the grass. Every aspect of her life is governed by the dictates of the perpetrator.

Spiritual abuse is often described as requiring the victim to participate in religious activities that are inappropriate, or against her beliefs. The victim of spiritual abuse may not be allowed to worship in freedom or perform ministry in areas she may have been active in for a long time. Some abusers may purposely intimidate the victims by misquoting or "mischaracterizing the Scriptures to assert his beliefs or to provide justification for his actions, and behaviors."

Verbal abuse may include the perpetrator "shouting, calling the victim inappropriate names, threatening to hurt or kill the victim and the children, laughing or making fun of the victim" (Domestic Abuse Information 2006, www.hiddenhurt.co.uk!Types/faces.htm). Verbal abuse is also abusive behavior that can cause damage to the victim's sense of self-worth and perpetuate feelings of hopelessness and helplessness.

Below are other 'red flags' that you are in an emotionally abusive relationship:

- You find yourself altering your behavior or changing who you are to "make your loved one happy"
- You find yourself walking on eggshells to avoid upsetting your loved one
- Your feelings and opinions are rarely validated
- You cannot reasonably discuss your concerns about the relationship without having a "blowout"
- You find yourself constantly "replaying" in your mind the hurtful things they said and wish you'd had a "better response"

God's Compassion Towards Me

- As much as you try to please your partner, they are "never satisfied"
- Your partner "has a problem" with everyone you hold dear – subsequently, you isolate yourself from loved ones in order to "make your partner happy"
- You have a difficult time expressing your independent thought, expressions or ideas for fear of being ridiculed

As Christians, we hold firm and true that the Bible holds everything we need to live a full, joyful and meaning life. 2 Timothy 3:16-17 tells us,

> *"All scripture is given by inspiration of God, and is profitable for doctrine, for reproof, for correction, for instruction in righteousness: That the man of God may be perfect, thoroughly furnished unto all good works."*

Secondly, we must believe that we have the ability to overcome the cycle of dysfunction, abuse, low self-worth, etc., when we exercise our faith and put our trust in God. 2 Peter 1:3 tells us,

> *"According as his divine power hath given unto us all things that pertain unto life and godliness, through the knowledge of him that hath called us to glory and virtue:"*

"Change" first starts in the mind. Ephesians 4:23-24 tells us that we must be "renewed in the spirit of your mind",

> *"And be renewed in the spirit of your mind; And that ye put on the new man, which after God is created in righteousness and true holiness."*

The renewal of the "spirit of your mind" means that we are to take on the "mind of Christ" (1 Corinthians 2:16). This means that our

Chapter 5: It's Never Too Late

desire is to think, see and speak as Jesus would. In order to see real change in our lives, we must "get out of our feelings" (how we see ourselves) and learn how to speak life, joy, peace and victory in our life! This can only happen when we ask God to transform our minds from carnal to spiritual (see Romans 8:6).

So, if we are diligent and we add that diligence to our faith, we will grow even more in the knowledge of Christ. The more we know and are obedient to Him, the more He will give us life and godliness (and will eventually move away the cycle of dysfunction, hurt, etc.,). The path to wholeness and completion won't be easy. It will require faith, effort, and determination – but it is not impossible. Philippians 3:13 says,

> *"Brethren, I count not myself to have apprehended: but this one thing I do, forgetting those things which are behind, and reaching forth unto those things which are before,"*

It is in God's perfect will that you live according to His purpose. He has given you everything you need to overcome Satan. You only have to exercise faith, "tap into God's power" and you will see the change in your life. God has empowered you (and you carry the authority of God) to bring under subjection whatever issue/challenge you're facing. Mark 11:23-24 tells us,

> *"For verily I say unto you, That whosoever shall say unto this mountain, Be thou removed, and be thou cast into the sea; and shall not doubt in his heart, but shall believe that those things which he saith shall come to pass; he shall have whatsoever he saith.*
>
> *Therefore I say unto you, What things soever ye desire, when ye pray, believe that ye receive them, and ye shall have them."*

God's Compassion Towards Me

Setting yourself free from trauma

satan likes to introduce trauma that typically begins in our childhood. This is because as a child, we don't yet possess the emotional and mental maturity to process what happened. Most of us did not get the help we needed at the time of the abuse because we were not taught how to communicate those feelings. These thoughts/feelings are buried somewhere in our psyche only to manifest itself into dysfunctional habits, thoughts and life choices. When we become an adult, we enter into toxic, drama-filled relationships. Finally, these dysfunctional habits, thoughts and relationships are typically perpetuated to the next generation.

If you've identified yourself in the above paragraph, then today is the day for you to gain freedom from emotional captivity. Below are some points that could be beneficial on your journey:

- Take notice of your patterns. If you find yourself in a cycle, find a counselor/Pastor that can help you break free from those destructive patterns.
- Take back your power to grow and evolve. Give yourself permission to remove yourself from things/people that fuel or trigger negative trauma.
- Make a determination as to who you allow to speak into your life. Learn to reject and/or ignore the opinions of people that "don't matter".
- Learn to abstain from making "emotional decisions". If you were to look back at all of your mistakes and regrets in life, I can say assuredly that 99% of your decision was made with emotion (and not logic).
- Speak life over yourself. Memorize/cite your favorite Bible verses that encourage your spirit. The level to which you "raise

Chapter 5: It's Never Too Late

your life" is largely dependent on a) how you "manage/assess" challenging situations, your "inner circle (e.g., friends/relationships), and what you speak. Proverbs 18:21 says,

> *"Death and life are in the power of the tongue: and they that love it shall eat the fruit thereof."*

It's not too late for a "do over."

All of us are a summation of decisions and choices we've made. Granted, we have made a lot of decisions that we wish we could take back. Often times, the enemy (satan), will use those poor decisions to oppress us, make us feel guilty or feel like there is no hope for our situation.

John 10:10 says,

> *"The thief cometh not, but for to steal, and to kill, and to destroy: I am come that they might have life, and that they might have it more abundantly."*

satan oftentimes will try to introduce trauma, abuse, violence, etc. in our childhood. The reason he does so is because very often these experiences will most likely be mishandled. We didn't have the number of resources you see today to deal with these issues when I was growing up. For many of us, we had to deal with the trauma the best way we could. For some, this meant abusing yourself (through drugs, alcohol or even worse, others). A child cannot properly process what has happened to them when they are abused or touched inappropriately. If that is not managed correctly, then that child will likely develop bad habits and/or begin making poor decisions. Poor decisions will eventually lead to even more poor decisions – thereby creating a cycle of dysfunction. This cycle of dysfunction (if not handled correctly) will affect generations to come.

The abuse and hurt that we've suffered come from satan – not the person that satan used. I know that what I'm about to say 'may not be popular' – however, if you are to become truly healed from your trauma, then please prayerfully consider what I'm about to say. The person that hurt or abused you is not your enemy – rather, "satan" (see 1 Peter 5:8).

We must understand that our fight/struggle is not with that individual person. Ephesians 6:12 says,

> *"For we wrestle not against flesh and blood, but against principalities, against powers, against the rulers of the darkness of this world, against spiritual wickedness in high places."*

Take your focus off of that person. Understand that your fight is not with them – they are not your enemy. Your enemy is satan. As I mentioned, since satan is a spiritual being, then the weapon to use against him must be spiritual as well – right?? You can't use a physical weapon (like a gun or sword) to fight a spiritual being (which is satan). 2 Corinthians 10:4 says,

> *"(For the weapons of our warfare are not carnal, but mighty through God to the pulling down of strong holds;)"*

Learn how to capture your thoughts.

When you find yourself triggered by something - practice how to counteract that thought with scripture (don't let that thought linger). 2 Corinthians 10:5 tells us, *"Casting down imaginations, and every high thing that exalteth itself against the knowledge of God, and bringing into captivity every thought to the obedience of Christ"*. Below are a few more examples:

> *"Finally, brethren, whatsoever things are true, whatsoever things are honest, whatsoever things are just, whatsoever things are pure,*

Chapter 5: It's Never Too Late

whatsoever things are lovely, whatsoever things are of good report; if there be any virtue, and if there be any praise, think on these things" Philippians 4:8

"For God hath not given us the spirit of fear; but of power, and of love, and of a sound mind." 2 Timothy 1:7

Take back your peace

The "peace" Jesus gives is grounded in God and not in circumstances.

- His peace cannot be obtained by self-effort; it is received by faith.
- Fear itself focuses on self and circumstances rather than on God. Focusing on God is central to everything Jesus said and did.

Philippians 4:6-7 tells us,

"Be careful for nothing; but in every thing by prayer and supplication with thanksgiving let your requests be made known unto God.

And the peace of God, which passeth all understanding, shall keep your hearts and minds through Christ Jesus."

John 16:33 tells us, *"These things I have spoken unto you, that in me ye might have peace. In the world ye shall have tribulation: but be of good cheer; I have overcome the world."*

Seek your own closure

Even though we may have been mistreated by someone, we don't seek retribution or rejoice/gloat when we see the people who mistreated us suffer misfortune. This is because we understand the principle of 'grace' – if it weren't for grace, we could've found ourselves in the same situation. Luke 6:28 tells us. *"Bless them that curse you, and pray for them which despitefully use you."* You cannot truly find closure for yourself by relishing in the hurt seen in others. Closure may be found by taking the hurt, trigger, abuse or violence to the altar and leave it there. We must be mindful that all of the pain and trauma we've experienced was crucified on the Cross with Jesus. Therefore, we shouldn't allow satan (or ourselves) to continue to resurrect that pain in our lives. We trust God that He sees our pain, is concerned about us (and more importantly), can take away the pain. We don't have to live with this pain for the rest of our lives. We don't have to allow the trauma of our past to oppress us. Jesus did not die on the cross for us to continue to live with the shame, guilt, or trauma of our past. Romans 5:20 tells us,

> *"Moreover the law entered, that the offence might abound. But where sin abounded, grace did much more abound."*

A biblical perspective on Forgiveness

This section on forgiveness/grace will be from the perspective on your finding closure and peace. We cannot find closure (much less demonstrate it to the world) until we have a proper understanding of these terms. It is my hope that the following paragraphs will help you on your journey towards forgiveness. Forgiveness can be described as, *"God gives us full pardon for missing the mark – He does not remind us of our faults."*

When God forgave you, He gave you full pardon - He did not remember your sin anymore. Psalm 103:12 tells us, *"As far as the east is from the west, so far hath he removed our transgressions from us."* We all have received the benefit of forgiveness for the wrong we've done.

Chapter 5: It's Never Too Late

However, one of the things that is most troubling to me is it appears as if the church had adopted the world-view on forgiveness and grace. The world has this "loophole" mentality or caveat when it comes to forgiveness:

- "I'll forgive you when it's convenient"
- "I reserve the right to bring back your fault(s) in front of your face when you make me mad"
- "God forgives - I don't"

The world will not show love or forgive how God shows. Though it may be painful, God expects us (as Christians) to show love to those that harmed us. For many, we might be the only representation of God's love that they will ever see. We all must understand that:

- Forgiveness does not mean what the person did to you was OK.
- Forgiveness does not mean your feelings about what was done to you is insignificant.
- Forgiveness does not mean that the person who harmed will not be held accountable.

Forgiveness means you've made a conscious decision to let go of that hurt/anger and have decided to seek/maintain "peace" (which is freedom from disturbances and distractions) for your life. I had such a personal experience in my second marriage to my then ex-husband. We had already been divorced for quite some time. But God told me to go back and tell him "I'm sorry". I didn't understand "why", and I initially rejected the notion. Out of obedience I went back to the person that physically, emotionally and mentally abused me for years to tell him "I'm sorry". When I met him and told him this, his response was, "For what? You didn't do anything." I replied, "I know, but I have to be obedient." I believe that God had me to do this so that I can be free from spiritual and emotional bondage.

It is your choice whether to forgive or not. However, if you continue to hang on to that unforgiveness it will continue to remind you of what that person did to you and how they made you feel. Eventually you will begin to seek unhealthy coping mechanisms to dull the pain. If this is you, find a counselor to help you navigate a course towards your inner healing. Holding on to unforgiveness gives satan a weapon to gain advantage over you.

A biblical perspective on Grace

Grace (definition): ***"God's favor toward the unworthy".***

Even if one were to ask (and receive) forgiveness, perhaps an even harder topic to broach is "Grace". For many, grace can be hard to receive and even harder to give. They can easily accept the fact that there is a "penalty" for doing wrong (they may say "Oops, my bad"), but a lot of times with "grace", there may not be any demonstrative "punishment". This is where most stumble because, in their eyes, it appears as if, "someone got away with something", "it was too easy" or "they didn't suffer enough". You don't have to be subject to this "every time I/they mess up, I/they must be punished" mentality. Psalms 37:24 says, *"Though he fall, he shall not be utterly cast down: for the LORD upholdeth him with his hand."*

Our desire should not be to "seek punishment" – for "we all have sinned and fallen short" (Romans 3:23). We ought to pray for those that harmed us. They might have been under the influence of satan (as we all have been at some point) and may not even know it. Jesus demonstrated this point when He asked God to forgive those that had Him crucified while He hung on the cross (Luke 23:34).

Chapter 5: It's Never Too Late

The world can only see the judgment (and not the grace) of God. This is because they have rejected the gift of salvation by God through Jesus Christ. John 3:19 explains this in greater detail,

> *"And this is the condemnation, that light is come into the world, and men loved darkness rather than light, because their deeds were evil."*

The world does not have a proper understanding of love, grace or forgiveness. They attack the idea of "grace" because they did not see the other person suffer the same way "they suffered". To see the offender accept "grace" makes it appear as though they "got off too easy".

We must show them that *"There is therefore now no condemnation to them which are in Christ Jesus"* (Romans 8:1). If you are given the opportunity to show grace to someone grace – do so. You might be the only representation of grace they see. Grace will show them that there are so many opportunities available for healing, deliverance, and blessings. God's grace and your faith must be combined in order to see the manifest power of God in your life. It is in God's nature to bless you.

God's Compassion Towards Me

About Dr. Chlorine F. Wimberly

With over 25 years of experience in the field of mental and spiritual health, Dr. Chlorine F. Wimberly has established herself as a valued service provider for the community in which she serves. A licensed clinical social worker, Dr. Wimberly is the President and CEO of IRISE Counseling Services, LLC, where she offers professional mental health and therapeutic services to individuals and organizations. In addition to her private practice, Dr. Wimberly contracts with an adult day treatment center and volunteers at health care facilities. She has traveled to Haiti, Panama, and South Africa ministering to the spiritual and mental needs of others.

Dr. Wimberly holds a Bachelor of Science degree in social work from Marygrove College, a Master of Science in social work from Wayne State University, a Master of Arts in Pastoral Counseling, and a Doctor of Divinity from Ashland Theological Seminary.

This chapter is an excerpt from Dr. Wimberly's dissertation entitled *Domestic Violence: A Journey Toward Healing*. Used by permission.

To contact Dr. Wimberly:
cfwimberly@yahoo.com

Reflection

As we reflect upon the wisdom shared by these authors, we can each see ourselves in some part of this book. Allow God to minister to your heart, soul, and spirit as only He can. Remember, God heals, restores, and transforms through the compassion of clinicians.

Blessed be God, even the Father of our Lord Jesus Christ, the Father of mercies, and the God of all comfort; Who comforteth us in all our tribulation, that we may be able to comfort them which are in any trouble, by the comfort wherewith we ourselves are comforted of God. II Corinthians 1:3-4

Dr. Lisa H. Fuller

About the Editor, Dr. Lisa H Fuller

For more than 30-years, Dr. Lisa H. Fuller has practiced psychiatry in the greater Detroit area and surrounding states. Dr. Fuller is the CEO and Chief Medical Officer for Discern Life Consultants Health.

Not only is Dr. Fuller a physician but has also earned a Bachelor of Science degree in Chemistry, an Associate of Arts degree in Christian Leadership, and an honorary Doctorate in Divinity.

Dr. Lisa H. Fuller is an Ordained Apostle and the Founder and Overseer of Lisa H. Fuller Ministries and Christ's Arms Reaching Ministries which provides clean water sources, food, and education scholarships in Kenya and Liberia, Africa. Dr. Fuller has led mission teams on the continents of Africa, Asia, Europe, and North and Central America with a focus on crisis and trauma, leadership development, and spirituality. Dr. Fuller has been recognized for Outstanding Leadership in Global Missions, by Second Ebenezer Church led by Bishop Edgar L. Vann, Distinguished Servanthood by the Liberian Evangelical Baptist Convention (LEBCO) Ganta, Liberia, and Master Teacher and Humanitarian by the Rapid Response Chaplain Corps.

To contact Dr. Lisa H. Fuller visit

https://DrLisaHFuller.com/

https://LisaHFullerMinistries.org/

https://ChristsArmsReachingEverywhere.org/

https://LearnRealisticHabitsForTheFuture.com

https://DiscernLifeConsultants.com/

http://MissionsMindedBooks.com/

Scan to purchase books by
Dr. Lisa H. Fuller

Books by
Dr. Lisa H. Fuller

You Already Have All of the Tools That You Need Special Edition

Words of encouragement & inspiration to let you know God already gave you all of the tools that you need.

ISBN 13: 978-0-9754023-0-6
Paperback | Retail Price: $10.00

~*~

ISBN 13: 978-0-9754023-7-5
Ebook | Retail Price: $2.99

God is Love: I John 4:8b

God Is Love: I John 4:8b helps you to tell the children in your life Who God is and helps them to have a relationship with Jesus. Spend time together reading while also sharing your faith with your children, grandchildren, nieces, nephews, and neighbors. God Is Love: I John 4:8b allows you to leave a legacy of faith to your children and children's children. It is also great for children's church and Sunday school classes.

ISBN 13: 978-0-9754023-1-3
Paperback | Retail Price: $12.00

~*~

ISBN 13: 978-0-9754023-8-2
Ebook | Retail Price: $1.99

Dios Es Amor I Juan 4:8b

Dios es amor I Juan 4:8b es un libro para niños que demuestra el amor de Dios y les ayuda a recibir a Jesús como su Salvador personal.

ISBN 13: 978-0-9754023-5-1
Paperback | Retail Price: $12.00

~*~

ISBN 13: 979-8-218-23096-8
Ebook | Retail Price: $1.99

Missions Minded Manual

Everyone can benefit from insight, tools, and resources when serving in the ministry. The Missions Minded Manual equips you for your mission experience.

ISBN 13: 978-09754023-4-4
Paperback | Retail Price: $10.00

~*~

ISBN 13: 979-8-9886371-3-4
Ebook | Retail Price: $0.99

Missions Minded Journal

Document your ministry experience and faith walk every step along the way whether serving as part of your local church's mission team, in partnership with another ministry, a nonprofit organization, food bank, or as part of international missions.

ISBN 13: 978-09754023-3-7
Paperback | Retail Price: $10.00

COMING SOON

Missions Minded
Managing Anxiety While Serving

Anxiety, fear, depression, thoughts of not being able to complete the mission can and usually do appear at some point of the mission journey. Not only does Missions Minded: Managing Anxiety While Serving address managing anxiety on the mission field, but also while serving in various ministry capacities.

ISBN 13: 979-8-9886371-2-7
Paperback | Retail Price: $10.00
~*~
ISBN 13: 979-8-9886371-4-1
Ebook| Retail Price: $3.99

God's Compassion Towards Me

Mental illness is a real and serious disease. When mental and emotional trauma occurs, help is desperately needed. The World Health Organization estimates one in four people globally will experience mental illness in their lifetime. In God's Compassion Towards Me, five Spirit-filled professional mental health clinicians share their own stories and how God empowers them to help others.

ISBN 13: 978-0-9754023-6-8
Paperback | Retail Price: $20.00

ISBN 13: 979-8-9886371-1-0
Ebook | Retail Price: $3.99

God heals by signs, wonders, and miracles...
over time...by using clinicians.

www.ingramcontent.com/pod-product-compliance
Lightning Source LLC
Chambersburg PA
CBHW072101290426
44110CB00014B/1774